Get Your Life!

A Quick & Easy Guide to Help You Set Goals and Write Personal Vision & Mission Statements to Live the Life of Your Dreams

By Norissa Williams, PhD

TABLE OF CONTENTS

Each of us is a seed of divinely inspired possibility,
which when nurtured in its proper context
can and will grow into the fullest expression
of all we are supposed to become.

-African proverb

Introduction

Around the age of 14 I became passionate about the notion of, "living my life on purpose." I gravitated to books on the topic, reading the late Myles Monroe's, *"Maximizing Your Potential"* and, *"In Pursuit of Purpose."* This notion of self-actualization (i.e., living my life to its' fullest potential and being all that I could be) literally consumed me. So, though only a teen, I asked myself questions that would get me answers about what the purpose of my life was. It wasn't long before I decided that I was here, not only here to maximize my potential, but to also create opportunities for and encourage the same in others.

I had big dreams. These dreams included community empowerment—giving back and helping those most in need. In keeping with those dreams I did as I was supposed to do to get where I wanted to get. I graduated high school, got a Bachelor's degree and also obtained a Masters degree by the age of 23. Not more than two or three months later I had gotten a great job and had gotten married. My life was going as planned.

However, it wasn't long before I realized that working 9-5 certainly wasn't the satisfaction I was looking for—nor was it anything I had previously dreamed. Beyond that I began to realize, for me, 9-5 living made for a passive existence. I don't know about you, but I'm not about punching the clock after a days shift to go home, cook, watch TV and sleep—only to have to turn around and do it again the next day. I recognize that this kind of life is fine for some and may even fit with their purpose, but for me—one who needs a certain amount of freedom and room for creativity, growth and change—it was depressing and I mentally kicked and screamed on a regular basis. I didn't have time to dream, far less act on those dreams. That just wasn't the life I had imagined and the gap between the life I wanted and the life I was living, became wider with each day.

I thought, "If this is what this 9-5 living is doing to me and I was actually in a career I liked, then this must be what others experience as well." Believing that my life was supposed to be about living to my full potential and inspiring that in others, I wanted to create a venue or springboard from which people could develop themselves and live an active existence in which they experience true life satisfaction.

Within that time I had gotten pregnant and had a baby. While on maternity leave I began to give serious thought to these things and craft ways in which I could address this inner restlessness. In just three months, I had not only given birth to my son, but I had conceived and given birth to new dreams as well. I returned to work having started a women's empowerment group. In essence, the vision of the group was to create, "a collective of women taking the self-actualization journey together" ...sharing ...networking...offering concrete and conceptual tools that contribute to one another's success. Thereafter, we would turn outward and share our strength with the larger community.

As part of this group I used a document that I initially

called a, "treatment plan." Traditionally, treatment plans are used in various therapeutic settings—most often in mental health settings. Clinicians use it in consultation with their clients. In general, it has four parts; 1) identification of problems 2) goals for treatment 3) methods for achieving those goals 4) as well as estimated time frames within which goals are expected to be met. It is used as much as a means to drive progress, as it is a means by which one can measure progress. This concept is the basis for the Empowered Life Plan presented to you in this book. However, the Empowered Life Plan was modified from the traditional treatment plan model and enhanced for the unique purposes of the group. It was designed to be a tool one uses to get themselves to their desired future—as opposed to dealing with a specific problem, at a specific time in our life as a treatment plan would. This plan should cause individuals not only to focus, but also to dream big and map out their never-ending journey towards self-actualization. As such in the Empowered Life Plan, vision, as well as mission statements are included, thereby also incorporating elements of a business plan.

It's been 9 years since the creation of this group and I'm often asked if the women in the group experienced what I imagined they would experience as part of the group. I always answer, "YES!" emphatically. We have members who have gone back to school and obtained PhDs (myself included), completed Bachelors degrees, started businesses, completed books, started families, changed careers, run for local office (and won), traveled internationally, etc.

I don't list, "accomplishments" because they define us or are markers of self-worth, but because these were goals that these women had, that for some reason or other they put aside, quieted or didn't act on. In fact, some of these women had never even dreamed as big. Yet and still, I think the biggest successes are that in the end we had women that were happy with their lives, feeling contented as they felt a oneness between the woman they wanted to be and the woman they actually were. The Empowered Life Plan was a large part of this success. It is my sincere hope and firm belief that this book can help you do the same—whether you are a man or woman.

As you complete this plan you are asked to think vastly about the kind of life you would like to live. At the end of your days, how would you like your life to be summed up? What are the parts that make up the collage of your life? What are your goals? What are the stepping-stones that will take you to your desired end, for each specific goal? What are the resources already at your disposal? What are the resources that you need to acquire? You are asked to think about these things as grandiose as you please, because these things are well within your reach.

This book is intended to be a guide that you use as you journal. Steps will be outlined in each chapter. At the conclusion of writing this plan, you will have written a vision and mission statement for your life. In addition, you will have identified both long and short-term goals and have identified objectives. Your process will begin with visualization and end with the completion of an entire, typed *Empowered Life Plan.* Please read through the Chapters 1-4 once before beginning so you can have a holistic picture of what is expected of you.

This book is offered to you from a place of my seeking to be aligned with the purpose of my life, which as stated earlier, is to, *"create opportunities for and remove impediments to individuals ability to self-actualize".* So, with all sincerity, I wish you much success on your journey to self-actualization and hope that you find this tool useful. Most of all, I wish you full-life satisfaction.

CHAPTER 1

WRITING YOUR VISION STATEMENT

What is the desired landscape of your life? Do you know? Like, really *really* know?? If you've answered, "Yes" then, Great! Go you! This can be a tool to help you further refine these things as you think about the more finite pieces—the nuts and bolts—to pull this thing together. If you were luke-warm or outright answered, "No" you're still in a good place, because you're here. A few of the women in the group, who went on to accomplish many of their goals, might be able to relate to this. Nonetheless, like those women, you're in a great place because you're thinking about it and this is evidence enough that you have begun your journey. Nonetheless, this process is important because it is only after we have made our vision clear to ourselves that we can organize our efforts and behaviors around making these things reality.

In writing your *Empowered Life Plan* you will begin with writing a vision statement. Vision statements are often used in the introduction of a business plan. It describes the dream of the business or organization. In this context we are discussing the vision of your life. Therefore, when we say, "vision statement," we are referring to the written description of the desired landscape of your life. It is not centered on the process (i.e., specific goals and objectives) of what you want to do. It is the entire picture; a collage of what you hope your life to be. It should answer the following question, "If you were looking back at the end of your days, what would your desired life have looked like?"

Below, are a few processes that have the aim of helping you to think expansively about the answer to this question. Please go through each step, spending as much or as little time as you need to answer these questions.

***

I. **Activity:** *Creative Visualization*

The creative visualization process is one in which you use your imagination to visualize specific behaviors or events occurring in one's life. (Note: You can do one step per day. There is no rush in this process):

Answer the Question: *What makes me happy*?

a) *List these items.* You are encouraged to think about as many things as possible as we are multifaceted individuals. These things may include aesthetic items such as nice clothes, houses or travels. It may also include certain disciplines such as, exercising regularly, eating healthy or meditating regularly. It should also include growth aspirations, whether it is personal, spiritual and/or professional.

b) *Return to every item on your list.* Use your imagination to envision the lived experience of these things. Use your senses as well. *What does it look like? What does it feel like? What does it smell like? What does it taste like?* Ask these questions for each item listed. For example, if one of the items on your list were, "being physically fit" in imagining the lived experience of this, you might see yourself toned and feeling strong. Imagine yourself touching your biceps and admiring its definition, smiling as you look in the mirror because you look so good. You'll use these descriptors in writing your vision statement so that it is as vivid as possible.

Go all the way with this creative visualization process. For example you may have listed, "helping people" as something that makes you happy. It makes you feel good. Currently, you do it with people in your life and participate in many community service activities. You have already thought about what it feels like in the present, but does this expression differ in the future? Would you like to do this professionally? What does it look like in the future? Are you helping people in an academic setting? Teaching? Tutoring? Or are you a social worker, helping people access needed resources in the community? Or do you work in a clinical capacity? Whatever you list, it is important that you be as specific about these things as possible. Treat it like an unfamiliar rock that intrigues you. Pick it up. Turn it over several times in your minds eye. Examine it from every angle and most importantly, allow your self to dream big.

c) *Put it all together.* Imagine what your day-to-day life looks like with the incorporation of all these things. What does it look like daily? Weekly? Monthly? Yearly? How do you feel? Take time to incorporate all the things you have listed. Have you included such things as getting married/growing in your marriage, becoming a mother/being a good mother, spending time with your extended family, being part of a church, joining a sorority, etc. Include the finite details in this visualization.

d) *Write*. If you have followed the previous steps, you have grist for the mill; meaning, you have the ingredients to write your vision statement. You can now begin to formulate these ideas into a written statement.

Pretend you are 80 years old. You have many years left to live, but you are in a retrospective state and are thinking about your life. You're happy with how it turned out.

In writing your statement you will speak in the present tense but as you visualize this, think from the perspective of your older self and how you would have assessed your life and what you would have wanted to happen. What kind of life did you live? Did you live, as you wanted? What did that look like? Tell this story.

Each person's statement will look different. However, the following example offers an idea of how it can start:

"I am a strong, compassionate and beautiful/handsome woman/man. My family and friends have been able to count on me in times of need. Though I am a source of strength and support for others, I know how to attend to my own needs, as well. I have done that for myself for many years and am emotionally healthy as a result. I am very satisfied with life...I have climbed to the top of the ladder in corporate America. The excellence of my work has always spoken for itself...I am well respected in the community. In addition to achieving all my professional pursuits, I have made a life of helping those in need...I exercise regularly and eat nutritiously. I have optimal health..."

After having completed your vision statement you are ready to write your mission statement. However, before you go on, please take time to reflect on whether or not you thought as expansively as you could have. As a teen, the pastor of the church I attended pointed out that the word vision begins with a, "V". He said that if you think about that "V" you would see that the base of the letter is closed. Think of that as your bird's eye, present view. However, the arms or lines that make it a, "V" don't touch. In fact, if you took a ruler and extended that V on this page or any other surface, the edges will never touch. They only get more expansive—expansive enough to hold all that you put in it. So it should be with your life's vision. There are no limits. The possibilities are endless. Think BIG!

Chapter 2

Writing Your Mission Statement

You have now written your vision statement. It describes the landscape of your desired life. You are now poised to write your mission statement. Mission statements are different from vision statements as they answer the question of what the purpose of your life is (*why you exist*)—as opposed to what it looks like. They are also different from vision statements in that they are more specific. They are shorter and focus on the present as opposed to the future.

In business, mission statements are used to keep the business focused. Employees can refer to it as a reference point for what they are supposed to be doing. In so doing, it drives the work done under the auspices of the business. In addition, it helps administrators plan.

Imagine there was a paper company in your local neighborhood. They were founded with a passion for enabling the transmission of ideas via the written word. They sold paper, printed books, magazines, etc. Then one day, they were approached by a national company that asked them to sell art supplies—offering a great incentive to do so. Seeing it as a potentially lucrative venture and not that far off from what they do, they began to sell art supplies. This is not their area of expertise. However, it becomes very lucrative and soon people don't buy paper supplies from them anymore. They begin to focus their efforts on making themselves more competitive in the art supply market. Yes, they are doing well financially but after some time the founder of this business begins to experience a level of dissatisfaction. He/she is no longer doing what once motivated them—enabling the transmission of ideas via the written word through providing paper supplies at an affordable price.

What happened here? The answer is simple. The owner veered from the mission of his/her business in pursuit of profit. In fact, there was no articulated mission that could have been referenced when they were making business decisions. You may have read this thinking the outcome wasn't so bad. While its true because more money was made, it could have worked in the reverse. However, it is important to note that the owner had returned to a state of dissatisfaction, as there was now a divide between what the owner wanted to do and what they were actually doing. Having a clear mission statement could have made it so that when given the opportunity to expand, the owner could have referenced the mission statement and asked, "Is this consistent with the reason for which I started this business?" If the answer was no, the new venture shouldn't have been pursued.

Your response to the given scenario and assessment of whether the outcome was good or bad is based on what your values are. If your values are profit, then fine. The owner made out well. If your values are life satisfaction and living your dream, then the owner is in need of a compass, or mission statement, to direct them back towards living a life of meaning.

Personal mission statements accomplish the same thing. It identifies one's purpose and briefly states the way in which you will accomplish it. In essence, it answers the question of what you do, how you do it and why do it. It should be no more than a few sentences. It should be easily understood, and you should be able to recite it.

The following processes will help you in writing one.

***

I. Activity: *Journal*

Referring to the things you listed in the creative visualization process used for writing your vision statement, answer the following questions in a very meditative and reflective mode:

a) *What are you passionate about?* What are the things that excite you and/or leave you with a great sense of satisfaction? Think about these things for a while.

Are there *common themes* among the things listed? If so, what are they? You might have listed that you enjoy working in food pantries, cooking for people, volunteering in the hospital, etc. A common theme in this instance might be service.

Can any of the themes you listed be modified and made more specific? For example, though you have described service as an overarching theme, you might find that it is not just service that excites you. Service to immigrant communities might more accurately define what you are passionate about.

b) *Further define your passions.* Styling hair might excite you and be your passion. However, you can be more specific and say that you are passionate about making people feel as beautiful outside as they are inside. Maybe you are more interested in the artistry of it and your passion is expressing yourself creatively through styling hair. One might also be more interested in, "styling hair and making people feel beautiful at affordable prices." There is a clear distinction between the three. These clear definitions are important.

Further examples are: teaching people about nutrition and good health practices, helping people to save money, organizing documents, helping small businesses gain notoriety, etc.

Teaching might have been listed as a goal. It can be made more specific by asking the questions: What do I like to teach? Is it academic subjects or social skill building like peer relations, etc.? Take it further by asking, who do I like to teach? In the previous example, one might have found, "Teaching teenagers about nutrition and good health practices," might have been the epitome of what they really mean. Dig deep, be specific and use short phrases.

c) *Write your mission statement.* At this point you should have a few short phrases that describe the things that you are passionate about, would like to do with your life and believe may be your purpose. Review the list and ask yourself whether or not there are things on this list that you like to do, but might not be driving passions of your life? If they do not meet the criteria, cross them off the list. Continue to be mindful of themes that exist among the things listed.

Are there any things on your list that may be truncated? Is there a statement that can be made that encompasses as many of these things as possible? For example, the mission statement for my life reads: *To create opportunities for and remove impediments to individual's ability to self-actualize through teaching, writing, research, counseling and social programs.* This statement encompasses all that I want to do in life. I want to write books, teach psychology and social sciences, motivational speaking/teaching, develop programs in the community (American inner cities as well as abroad), be a researcher, help make cultural psychology more mainstream, inspire people to live their dreams, life coach, counsel, etc.

All that I want to do is encompassed under the umbrella of this mission statement. All these activities serve to "create opportunities for and remove impediments to individuals abilities to self actualize". Each activity can be categorized under the broader categories of, teaching, writing, counseling and social programs.

In addition, though it may not be apparent to the observer, the motivation behind all the things that I have listed is that I really enjoying helping people to live their dreams (aka, self-actualize). This applies in any context whether it is among my peers, with my child, extended family, in the school context, the creation of a women's group or anything else.

The benefit of having such a statement is that as a psychologist, having obtained a terminal degree in my field, I'm often approached with opportunities to write things, speak, etc. Whenever opportunities come my way I mentally reference them against my mission statement and see whether it fits with the ideals I have for my life. If they don't fit, I say no. If they vibe with my mission statement, I say yes, as my ultimate goal is full life satisfaction, being aligned with my purpose and being true to myself.

While this process is not so rigid that a mission statement cannot later be changed or revised, you want to create something now that will stick. As such, in writing this statement find the balance between thinking and writing broadly, while also being specific and focused.

After you have come up with a phrase that encompasses everything that you desire to do, write it down. Then, ask yourself:

1. Does this statement encompass all the things that I want to do?
2. Does it describe my reason for existence?
3. Does it describe how I will do it?
4. Does it describe why?
5. Is it easily recited?

Take time to make sure all these things are attended to in your mission statement. After you have completed both your mission and vision statements you can move on with the more active part of the Empowered Life Plan. In the next chapter we will define your goals and objectives.

CHAPTER 3

DETAILING GOALS AND OBJECTIVES

"Rome was not built in one day"~ John Heywood
"The journey of a thousand miles begins with one step"
~Lao Tzu

At this point you have both your vision statement and your mission statement. Now it's time to write goals and objectives. In order for us to begin doing so, we must first identify where we are.

***

1. Activity: *Journal*

a) ***The Journey.*** Refer to your vision statement. Go through every sentence. You wrote about things that you would like to see happen in your life. In some areas, a gap exists between where you are and where you want to be. What is this gap? **The task of this step is to identify the gaps that exist between where you are and where you want to be.** For example, you might have listed that you have the highest degree possible in your desired field, but currently, you are about two degrees short. Using your journal, identify the areas in which gaps exist. In the example just mentioned, the "gap" is a gap in education. However, you can address less concrete things, as well. You might want to be emotionally whole.

However, you know you have many wounds that need healing. The gap here would be, a need for healing.

You can title this list, *The Journey*. We are entitling it this, as it lays out for us the terrain that must be traveled to get from point A (where we are) to point B (where we want to be in time).

b) **The Path**. This step is simple. Go through the things you listed in the previous step. In, "step a" you identified areas in which gaps exists between your present state and the vision that you have for yourself. In order to address these things you will have to identify goals for yourself. How are you going to get you where you want to be? **The task of this step is to identify goals.** For example, in your vision you speak Spanish. However, you don't yet. Your goal is to learn Spanish.

c) **Stepping Stones**. You have become familiar with the terrain—creating a clear image of the journey you must take. In addition, you have narrowed your focus and become familiar with the individualized path you have to take to get you from point a to point b. You now have to look at the stepping-stones along the path. These are the steps you must take to advance you along the path. You can also call them, objectives or action steps. **The task of this step is to identify your objectives/action steps.** What are the stepping-stones that will take you along your path?

Objectives are the clear, specific steps that we must take in order to accomplish our goals. They must be measurable and time limited. For example if your goal is:

Goal: Learn Spanish
Objectives may be:

1. Find a low cost Spanish class in my community within the <u>next two months.</u>
2. Begin taking Spanish classes within the next <u>six months</u>
3. Learn at least conversational Spanish <u>within the next year.</u>

Our Goals may be things we hope to accomplish within the next twenty years. Don't feel pressured to make everything happen this year. Be realistic with yourself. It is a journey; making it time limited and measurable just makes it so that you will be actively working towards it and can mark your progress. (Before continuing to the next chapter, please see the first Bonus Chapter; *Chapter 7: Two Fun Facts About the Brain That Can Help or Hinder Goal Accomplishment.*)

In considering your objectives/stepping stones you will want to consider and make a list of your internal resources or personal strengths. What are those inherent characteristics that you have that will make you successful at your goals?

In addition, you want to consider your external resources. Who and what are your external resources? Include those individuals, groups and organizations that you are affiliated with that will be useful to you as you go on your journey—whether it be for networking purposes or personal support.

Considering these things, for each objective, may cause you to realize yet more objectives. For example, you may not have any groups to which you belong that may help you. You might need to add that as an objective. You might need to be less susceptible to other people's opinions. Conversely, thinking of your resources may help you in eliciting people to help keep you accountable for certain things you want to do. Accountability planning is the subject of the following chapter.

CHAPTER 4

CREATING AN ACCOUNTABILITY PLAN

Not to long ago I took a picture of myself and balked when I looked at it. "OMG!" I thought, mentally clutching my pearls. "I can't be this fat!" Truth be told this was nothing new to me. I had gained 10 pounds in the earlier part of the year. Then I lost a few, gained it back, lost it again and gained it right back. So here I was again, disgusted and ready to do something about it.

"No. For real... This is ridiculous! I'm going home tonight and I'm going to get on that air climber and go for thirty...NO! FORTY-FIVE minutes!!" The rest of the evening I plotted what else I would do to lose this weight—maybe go back on that juice fast, start eating breakfast, stop skipping meals, cooking at home, etc. After devising a plan I smiled smugly thinking, "You're so bad a**." I had this!

Three hours later I walked in the house still semi revved up. However, with each step towards my bedroom (where I keep my make-shift gym) I lost more gumption to do any physical activity and finally thought, "*Eh...tomorrow...*"

Now, truthfully, how many times have you done that? How many sweet goals rest on the promises of tomorrow? Except...one tomorrow turns into 50 tomorrow's and it's only until the next horrific picture you see that you gasp and think, "I HAVE to do something about this!"

In contrast, some weeks before I had come across a blog post shared casually on face book. A woman in the UK drank 12 glasses of water for 28 days and experienced miraculous health benefits. On top of that, her before picture looked 10 years older than her after picture. When I saw this I thought, "I want to do this. I *NEED* to do this!" I forwarded the article to my best friend and asked if she was in? She was. For 30 days we drank approximately 96 ounces a day, give or take a few (we're not perfect). Each day we checked in. In between our regular texts we'd ask each other, "How much did you drink today?" We congratulated each other when we were on target, "Go 'head girl! Look at you!" When we weren't, we'd give tips to the other. However, the most important part of this shared accountability was that we each got motivated from the check in's and would run to get more water, seeking to fill our daily quota's. It was all done in a loving, non-competitive way. The point is, there is nothing like having an accountability partner as you make goals and set out to accomplish things in life. In fact, this is how I accomplish most tasks in life and I encourage you to do the same.

There are a few things you want to think about when choosing an accountability partner. Look at your goals and objectives. Think about the ones that you can do alone and the ones you might need someone to shoulder the challenge with. For the ones you opt to have an accountability partner for (and I would applaud you, if you chose all!) think of who might be best suited to assist you. The best partner might be one who is pursuing a similar goal. This helps because as they think of their goals they will also think of you and check in more regularly. In addition, the shared joy of accomplishment may make it a sweeter experience. As well as they can share pitfalls, lessons learned and vice versa. In addition, you want someone who is objective, nonjudgmental and won't shame you if or when you fall off track. Unless of course, you're a glutton for punishment and one for whom that kind of help is useful. However, if based on your personality and style, you opt for someone less intense just ensure that they are fully knowledgeable of what it is you are trying to accomplish and why. Also make sure you clearly define the kind of help you need from them.

***

Once you've selected your accountability partner:

1. Inform them of your plan (inclusive of your mission and vision statements, goals and objectives). Your partner needs to be invested. In addition, they may be able to suggest objectives and or/ resources you hadn't thought of.

2. Make sure your goals are broken up into objectives that are measurable. Let your partner know the time frame you expected to accomplish your goals.

3. Decide the kind of help you want from your partner and let them know in clear and certain terms.

4. Put the plan in action. You should have discussed the regularity with which you would have checked in with each other about your goals.

5. Check in regularly. Modify goals and accountability partnering as you go along and as is suitable for the two of you.

Having someone you know you are accountable to defeats the resident procrastinator within that says, "You know what...*I'll do it tomorrow.*"

An alternative to having an accountability partner is having an accountability group. As stated in the opening of this book, this plan was first used with a women's empowerment group. In our group, each member was assigned a personal accountability partner (using the steps above), but the larger group served as an accountability group as well. In group meetings, we regularly brought our plans in and discussed them. The other women in the group often served as a resource, helping each other reach their desired end. These women had multiple resources that were of benefit to other group members. These resources included knowledge of systems and enterprises one might need to access, referrals for professional services or even just fresh ideas. As needed, if a woman had a stuck point as she went about trying to accomplish her goals she would bring it to the group and the women in the group would help brainstorm solutions to the issue brought to the group. Once, in a "stuck point," session I presented my marketing plan to the group. I thought I had it all figured out. However, when the women heard the ideas they were able to offer useful advice. They all chipped in ideas and offered to speak to people they knew on my behalf. It was a very beneficial process. When one of the members ran for the school board, and later local office, a few of us chipped in to help with door-to-door campaigning, making calls and other efforts. (For tips on how to start an empowerment circle of your own, see the second bonus chapter added for your benefit. *Chapter 8: Starting an Empowerment Circle of Your Own).*

You can use your Empowered Life Plan in a group setting or you can choose to do it with just one partner. What is important in this step is that you partner with someone to help make you accountable for the changes you say you want to make in your life because as they say, there is strength in numbers.

Here is an example of what goals and objectives with an accountability partner might look like:

Goal: Lose weight
Objectives:
1. Document food intake daily.
2. Switch to wheat bread instead of white bread.
3. Use brown sugar instead of white sugar.
4. Join Weight Watchers.
5. Join a local gym.

You've reviewed your goals and objectives and determined you may be able to work well independently on finding a Weight Watchers and gym, as well as switching to wheat bread and brown sugar. However, you're not disciplined enough to regularly document your food intake. A partner may be of assistance here. Discuss it and develop a plan.

Objectives:
1. Document food intake daily. *(You would choose one of the following or more:)*

*Michelle will text me daily to see whether or not I

have documented my daily intake OR

*I will show Michelle my daily intake sheets on a weekly basis OR

*Michelle will create a grid for me to daily document my intake OR

*Michelle will help me research other weight loss alternatives.

2. Switch to wheat bread instead of white bread.
3. Use brown sugar instead of white sugar.
4. Join Weight Watchers.
5. Join a local gym.

Let's be honest and open. Let's lay down our defenses and be open to assistance. Finally, let's be enthusiastic.

CHAPTER 5

TYPING UP YOUR PLAN

Congratulations!! You have arrived at a very pivotal point in this process. In fact, you've already done all of the work. You will now take your journal and sit at your computer and type this up as a contract for yourself. The only things you need to include in this typed version are, your vision statement, mission statement, goals and objectives (inclusive of things your accountability partner will help you do). The other things were aids used to help you get to the final document.

There are different ways you can choose to do this. You can do an old-fashioned word document with the headings; vision statement, mission statement, goals, and objectives. Include accountability partner activities in your objectives.

You can also create an excel spreadsheet where you enter your goals and objectives. Columns could be; goals, objectives/action steps, target date, responsible parties (include accountability partners here) and progress to date.

Use whatever format is most suitable for your personality and enables you to look at your goals and objectives with ease.

CHAPTER 6

ASSESSMENT AND REFLECTION

After typing and printing this document you are asked to refer to it every now and again to chart your progress. When I initially began to use this document I referred to it at central points in the year. My birthday happens to fall halfway through the year. As such I would look at it then and note whether or not I had accomplished goals I set in a particular time frame. I would also come back to it at the start of the new-year.

You can choose to do it yearly, bi-annually or quarterly. The reflection and self-assessment period is left to your discretion based on your needs, goals and personal preferences. When you do reflect, you will find that sometimes it is necessary to modify goals. You change, so some of your goals may change as well. At times there will be large things that you might cross off the list— having completed them. Other times you will just make minor adjustments. There might also be times when there will be things you had forgotten were on the list. You will be motivated again to pursue them or to discontinue them. What is most important is that you make sure to celebrate your successes along the way!! (For more ideas on celebrating mini successes, see the bonus chapter added for your benefit. *Chapter 9: Reframing Success: Mini-Goal Celebrations*).

CHAPTER 7

TWO FUN FACTS ABOUT THE BRAIN THAT CAN HELP OR HINDER GOAL ACCOMPLISHMENT

"I'm going to save for the down payment of a house."
"I'm going to build a six-month emergency fund."
"I'm going to lose 20 pounds."

And so goes the goals we set for ourselves...

If I asked you to look at these goals with a critical eye, could you see the self- sabotaging nature of these goals? In theory they look just fine, but what most people don't realize is that there is a science to goal setting and these lofty aims—causing us to run headfirst into our own failure—just ain't it!

Goals should be clear, concise, measureable and most of all OBTAINABLE! How much are you saving for that down payment? In how much time? What are the concrete action steps that will enable this? And what time, social and financial resources do you have to make this a reality? In addition to these answering these questions— each worthy of a chapter of their own—I'll share a little with you of what the greats know as it pertains to goal setting.

1. **Goals should be as small as possible.** Dr. Robert Maurer, in his book, *"One Small Step Can Change your Life: The Kaizen Way,"* educates us on the way the brain works. Change is scary. When we tell our brains that we are going to do something new such as, "start exercising," our brain perceives such stark change as a threat to our current state of balance. As such, our, "fight or flight," response kicks in. So, sometimes, one's response may be to put off exercising for days, weeks—even years. One might even provide a million legitimate excuses for why they can't exercise. "I don't have the time. I can't afford a gym. And for crying out loud, "Who's gonna watch the kids?!"

Dr. Maurer advises that we make goals as small as possible. As opposed to saying, "I'm going to run 3 miles a day,"—which is still more concrete and measurable than, "I'm going to start exercising,"—say, "I'm going to walk in place 1 minute a day." In so doing we override our natural tendency for the, "fight or flight," response. Walking in place a minute a day is not threatening. As such, we're more likely to do it. In so doing the probability is that you'll surpass that minute and walk five, ten—and in time—even thirty minutes a day.

2. **Visualize yourself accomplishing your goals.** Once you have "micro'ed" your goals (that is, made them as small as possible), you're ready for the following step. Visualize yourself accomplishing these goals. See yourself doing each of these steps with ease. Experience every aspect of it. What does it look like? Feel like? Or smell like? Live its' reality, mentally.

Law of Attraction proponents are familiar with this, but science has also come to agree. Cognitive Psychologist, Dr. Colleen Seifert, calls this phenomenon, "predictive encoding."

When you practice visualizing a thing, your brain does not distinguish reality from fanciful imaginings—neural pathways are created nonetheless. As such, your brain will act as though it has happened and is an actual habit, not only overriding one's, "fight or flight," response but also augmenting one's ability to notice when they are provided with opportunities to act on their "habits".

If you don't believe it, try it!

CHAPTER 8

7 TIPS TO START YOUR OWN EMPOWERMENT CIRCLE

As I've told you, almost a decade ago I found myself less than enthused with the real world. It was a monotonous kind of existence—get up, eat breakfast, go to work, come home, eat, sleep, rinse and repeat. Prior to, I was a student. In those days I had all these dreams about what I wanted my life to be and all these amazing goals, but here I was bored and not really sure what I had to look forward to. And goals? What goals? 9-5 living provoked a passive kind of existence with only enough energy for the next day.

I began to think if I feel this way, there must be others who do too. With this inkling I decided to start a "Women's Empowerment Group," (i.e., a sister circle). I wanted to create an intimate space where women could gather to network and share resources—inspiring each other to revive old goals, make new ones and move towards them.

Almost 9 years later, we're still together. Since that time, I've obtained a doctoral degree. Another woman, who was a teenage mom, went back to school, completed her Bachelor's and just finished a law degree. Three of us write for the blog *thefrugalfeminista.com*, while there are others who've started businesses, gotten married, had children and shoot...there's even a County Legislator among us, now.

On a monthly basis, I set up numerous workshops for the women—some I conducted, some I invited special guests. However, the truth of the matter is that there was magic happening just because we were together. "Oh wow, look at you, you inspire me. I want to be my best too," and that was the aim of the group as I fully believe as Marianne Williamson said, "As we let our light shine, we unconsciously give others permission to do the same."

Now it's time for you to start your own empowerment circle! Our group had a general focus, "empowerment in every aspect of our lives," but you can start one around a particular topic such as home ownership, single motherhood, getting out of debt or entrepreneurship. Below are a few tips based on my tenure as group leader.

1. Decide how regularly you want to meet. Weekly? Monthly? Quarterly?

2. Determine what the mission of your group is. Answer the question of why you exist. It serves as an anchor for who you invite to the group and the regular activities you participate in.

3. Be picky about who you invite to the group. You want people to get along, as well as you want every one to feel comfortable and safe.

4. Keep the group intimate. I recommend 8-12 people. Not every one will come to every meeting, so it's nice to invite enough that there are at least 5 people each meeting, but not so many that you lose your intimacy.

5. Decide where you will meet. We met monthly at different peoples homes. Either the host provides all the refreshments or we do pot lock. However, you could also choose coffee shops, restaurants, bookstores or reserve rooms in your public library. Whatever, works for you— just make sure you can hear each other.

6. Decide the kinds of things you want to happen in your group. Volunteer and charity activities, anyone? Or would you rather focus on your own personal development—using self-help books or solely your empowerment plans. There is no right or wrong answer.

7. Keep every one motivated. Sometimes we can't see the forest for the trees, so at minimum on a yearly basis review individual and group goals and mark progress. People are often surprised with their progress, as well as they are motivated when they see where they've fallen short. Allow space and time for members to discuss, "stuck points" as it pertains to their empowerment plans. Make sure the culture of the group is one in which people are motivated to help each other reach their dreams.

In conclusion, I'd like to share the most surprising thing I learned while coordinating my empowerment circle. In an interview for a blog I was asked, **"As a leader what was the most surprising thing you've learned in your own journey with this group?"** I answered, "I'm a very structured person. While, I do think the group exists this many years later because of this, I've learned that this groups' success has less to do with 'structure,' and more to do with atmosphere. It's funny, because I used to put a lot of time in with regards to planning our sessions, 'what are we going to do? What are we going to talk about?' but what I learned is that this group is who they are just because we are together. That's it...just because we are together. One of our guiding philosophies is a quote from Marianne Williamson, 'When we let our light shine, we unconsciously give others permission to do the same.' We are who we are because members look at each other, and in essence are given, "permission to do the same."

I offer that nugget of information as I encourage you to realize that starting a group like this expands each person's support system. Members benefit as they have a personal cheering squad while they pursue their dreams, and at other times, a shoulder to cry on as members join arms and mourn with each other when they have lost.

CHAPTER 9

REFRAMING SUCCESS: MINI GOAL CELEBRATIONS

A psychologist friend of mine—who is known for his tenacity—was sharing a bit of the first phase of his career development journey with me. One blind to the behind-the-scenes lives of pre-tenured professors—in tenure track positions—might not imagine how real the pressure is. While it isn't quite the trading room floor of the New York Stock Exchange, it isn't a walk in the park either. There are pressures to teach, write, publish and secure grants in a short amount of time—never mind having a personal life.

In relaying the challenges of this academic grind, the good doctor shared with me that in his office he kept a canvas with paint and brushes. *With the submission of an article, a proposal, or a grant, he paints a stroke of color on the canvas.*

"Hmph! Intriguing!" I thought. Paint strokes didn't come after being awarded a grant or after a journal has accepted his article for publication—which is clearly the end goal—but strokes came with the acknowledgement and celebration of **effort**, while in "process," or *on the way* to his desired goal. We don't do that enough.

We often wait for some kind of external validation before we celebrate (or see the value in) the things we've done and learned en route to our goals. In a capitalist society, we're socialized to think in terms of "product," not, "process." What would happen if we more readily celebrated ourselves and our efforts _along_ the way?

Weight Watchers has it built into their system. You don't have to get to your 15-pound weight loss goal to celebrate. If you were shrewd and disciplined enough to have refrained from weight inducing food intake during the week, you're rewarded with a few delectable points with which you can splurge on foods of your choice at the end of the week. I've done it before. Not only does the success feel good, but celebrating my steps in the journey made me feel like, "Look at me! I can do this." In addition, it serves to self-correct in real time. Too much blankness on my friend's canvas motivates him to get back on his grind—to fill up that canvas.

It's probably not Weight Watchers or tenure-track professorship aspirations for you. Maybe it's finishing school, writing a book, watching your toddler grow or something as seemingly simple as making friends. In either scenario I encourage you to see value in all of it, not just accomplishment of the end goal. Sure, be productive. Have high standards, but focus on the quality of your effort—not solely numeric measures of success. In addition to seeing the canvas as a concrete way to celebrate effort and mini-goals, we can also think about this painted canvas as a metaphor for life. The many abstract colors that will fill this canvas—though they represent blood, sweat and tears—also represent how beautiful our lives are if we step back, not looking solely at individual strokes, but the collection of strokes that exemplify the many wins of our lives.

CONCLUSION

If you knew me personally then you would know that it is with great sincerity that I offer you appreciation for taking the time to read this book. I don't consider it an entitlement to be a part of your journey, but a privilege. You could have chosen any book.

I hope the processes you have learned or reviewed in this book become transferrable tools that you can apply in other areas in your life. I also hope that the practice of dreaming big, documenting your goals and successes and incorporating accountability partners into your life will be things that you use repeatedly on your journey.

If you would like to be in contact with me don't hesitate to email me atingdui@gmail.com. I do personal life coaching, psychotherapy and motivational speaking both face to face and through the use of technology. In addition, you can find my blog posts, of www.thefrugalfeminista.com, as I am one of the editors.

Also, this book is the first of a series of books entitled, "Tools for Living." Tools for living offers short self-help books to help you address specific issues or areas in your life. Look out for, "The Journey In" a 30-day book with journal prompts to help you take a closer look at who you are, why you are and where you're going. Each of these books seeks to help you release your own inner life coach. While assistance along life's journey in the form of counseling or a life coach is great, sometimes needed and encouraged, I want to offer tools to help you be your own life-coach!

Thanks again. I love you and happy living!

45730341R00028

Made in the USA
Middletown, DE
12 July 2017